fast
thinking:
selection
interview

PEARSON EDUCATION LIMITED

Head Office:
Edinburgh Gate
Harlow CM20 2JE
Tel: +44 (0)1279 623623
Fax: +44 (0)1279 431059

London Office:
128 Long Acre
London WC2E 9AN
Tel: +44 (0)20 7447 2000
Fax: +44 (0)20 7240 5771
Website: www.business-minds.com

First published in Great Britain in 2001

© Pearson Education Limited 2001

The right of Ros Jay to be identified as Author
of this Work has been asserted by her in accordance
with the Copyright, Designs and Patents Act 1988.

ISBN 0 273 65313 X

British Library Cataloguing in Publication Data
A CIP catalogue record for this book can be obtained from the British Library

10 9 8 7 6 5 4 3 2 1

Typeset by Pantek Arts Ltd, Maidstone, Kent.
Printed and bound in Great Britain by Ashford Colour Press, Hampshire

The Publishers' policy is to use paper manufactured from sustainable forests.

fast
thinking:
selection
interview

- ▶ **sift CVs fast**
- ▶ **interview with skill**
- ▶ **hire the right person**

by Ros Jay

contents

introduction 6

fast thinking gambles 10

1 your objective 14
Serious business 15

2 the vital documents 18
The job description 19
The employee specification 22

3 sifting the applications 28
Narrowing the field 28
Size isn't everything 32
Thanks but no thanks 33
Setting up the interviews 33

4 the questions 36
General questions 37
Individual questions 38
Who's asking the questions? 40

5 setting the scene 42
Prepare the room 43

Make them feel important   44
Help them relax   45

6 the interview   48
The interview structure   49
The techniques   50
Don't have opinions   56
Digging deeper   57
The legal position   61
Closing the interview   63

7 decision time   66
Your notes   67
Backing up your decision   69
Other considerations   75
Letting everyone know   77
What if you draw a blank?   79

8 other types of interview   82
Second interviews   82
Panel interviews   83
Interviewing internal applicants   84

interview in an evening   86

interview in an hour   88

introduction

Where did the time go? You advertised this post what seems like yesterday, but apparently it was a month ago. The interviews are supposed to be next week, and you haven't even started sifting through the applications yet, let alone compiling a list of likely applicants to interview. Or maybe you got that far, but the interviews are tomorrow and you can't even remember what the job description is.

You need a high-speed handbook to whisk you through the selection process at lightning speed, and still make sure that you end up selecting the right applicant. You wouldn't dream of picking a name out of a hat, but many managers might as well do, the way they go about selecting. No, you need to be fast but you also need to be smart. You've come to the right place.

Selection isn't just about chatting with a few applicants and then making a gut decision about who you want to appoint. It is a skilled process. You wouldn't buy a house without thinking hard about what you needed, what sort of potential the house should have, what features you would like but could manage without, and so on. A new employee may well, over time, cost the organisation as much as a new house, so the process warrants just as much thought and consideration.

That can seem like an impossible standard to meet when you're running out of time, but it can still be done. Maybe you've left the whole process to the last minute, or maybe it's just the interviews you're ill-prepared for. But even though the rest of your work is overtaking you, you can still make sure you select the best applicant. You just need:

 tips for getting on top of things fast

 shortcuts for avoiding any unnecessary work

 checklists to make sure you have the essentials covered

all put together clearly and simply. And short enough to read fast, of course.

And what if you really run out of time? If the interviews are tomorrow, you may just have to prepare for them this evening. But don't worry: it

Selection isn't just about chatting with a few applicants and then making a gut decision about who you want to appoint. It is a skilled process

can be done. At the back of the book you'll find a brief guide to preparing for interviews in only a few hours. In fact, if you have as little as an hour, it can still be done – as the turbo-charged one-hour version right at the end will show you. Now that really *is* working at the speed of life.

So relax. Take a deep breath. You may have left things late, but there's still time if you think smart and act fast. Now you know it can be done in sixty minutes, it makes even a few hours look like luxury, doesn't it? If you have a whole day for this, it's practically time to start bragging about how organised you are (so long as you don't brag for too long). So take the phone off the hook, make a cup of coffee, and let's get started.

work at the speed of life

This book will take you through the seven key stages of selection interviewing:

1 Before you can do anything else, you need to identify your objective. What exactly do you aim to achieve at the end of this process?

2 There are two key documents you need before you can possibly decide who is right for the job: the job description and the employee specification. So the next

chapter is all about what these documents look like and how you should use them.

3 If you haven't yet been through the applications, this is the next stage. Armed with your job description and employee specification, you need to slim down your pile of applications to a list of candidates worth interviewing.

4 Before the interview itself, you should prepare a set of questions to ask the candidates. So we'll look at the type of questions you need to ask.

5 You can't run selection interviews effectively in the wrong surroundings, or chaotic conditions. We'll look at the reasons why, and see how to set the scene for the interviews.

6 Now we come to the core of the process – the interviews themselves. We'll look at how to run the interview, how to glean the information you want from the interviewee, and how to tackle any thorny topics that may come up.

7 Finally, you have to make your decision. Which applicant will you give the job to? We'll look at how to choose the best candidate, how to check them out, and what to tell the rest of them.

We'll finish off with a quick look at other types of interviews, such as panel interviews and second interviews, since there are a few additional guidelines for these.

You may have left things late, but there's still time if you think smart and act fast

fast thinking
gambles

So, is it a good idea to race through the selection process at the speed of a cheetah, or is there a price to pay? Well, if you're doing it smart as well as fast – following the guidelines in this book – you can't go far wrong. You'll pick a candidate who is well up to the job (assuming the quality of the applications was good), and you should be very satisfied with them. The nagging doubt, though, is whether there might have been an even better candidate whom you missed. That's the gamble you take.

Most of the time, a well (if speedily) thought through selection process will identify the best candidate. But sometimes you may miss a better but less obvious candidate. Or you may know that there are two applicants you are finding it hard to choose between: more time would have meant more opportunity to work out which was the more suitable.

- The job description and the employee specification are your guidelines for picking the right candidate. They don't have to be long and wordy, but they do have to be accurate and informative. If you don't have time to prepare them effectively, you won't have a clear idea of what you are looking for. You may select a candidate who lacks a necessary skill, or who is unhappy when they find their job entails more time away from home than they realised.

- Sorting applications warrants a respectable time investment. Sure, you'll spot the blindingly good candidates pretty fast, along with the hopelessly unsuitable. But you may fail to identify the applicant who doesn't have all the qualifications you wanted, but who has flair that would more than make up for it.

- When you're under time pressure, you may miss details on the application form that would have been worth investigating. Perhaps there is a four-month gap in employment (you'll notice glaring gaps even at high speed), or a qualification in an unusual discipline, or a project they've been given that might indicate a particular talent, or a hobby that indicates a scientific bent. Following these leads could have revealed something very relevant – if only you'd had time to spot them.

- If your interviews give you the appearance of being unprepared, it will show you and your organisation in a poor light. So when both you and another company offer your best candidate a job, which one will they decide to take?

- When it is hard to choose between your top applicants, more time gives you more options – to follow up additional references, hold a second round of interviews, ask the candidates to take psychometric tests or whatever. When you're up against the clock, making the final decision can be tough.

Fast thinking will get you through the selection process at speed, and you'll end up with a good candidate – often the best one. That's most of the battle won. But if you want to be certain of picking the very best candidate every time, you'll need to find a little more time so you can ease up on the gas.

Fast thinking will get you through the selection process at speed, and you'll end up with a good candidate – often the best one

1 your objective

Have we got time for this? The interviews are twelve hours away – maybe less – and you're supposed to worry about objectives? You're just trying to get the post filled, surely?

Not quite. It's more specific than that. You are aiming to appoint the applicant who is most suitable for the job. And no, that's not the same thing. There are subtle but crucial differences. Suppose you are interviewing for an assistant chef in the canteen. You have two applicants. One is eighteen, and has a basic City & Guilds catering qualification. The other is twenty-eight, has a degree in food biology, and has run their own restaurant for four years. Which one is more suitable?

Presumably – all else being equal – the eighteen-year-old. It's no doubt just the job they're after, and they will enjoy it and work well. The twenty-eight-year-old, on the other hand, is odds on to leave through sheer boredom within the first month. So the better candidate, in terms of qualifications and potential, is not the more suitable one.

In real life, of course, the distinction is rarely so obvious. But the point is the same: you want the most *suitable* candidate – not necessarily the best-qualified, or the one with most experience. So you need to be clearly focused on your objective.

It's rather like buying a house. The most expensive house is not necessarily the best one for you. You might well be happier in the one that has a shorter walk to the station in the mornings, or that has a double garage that would make just the workshop you want, rather than have the three of you rattling around in a ten-bedroomed mansion.

SERIOUS BUSINESS

When time is tight, it's very easy to be drawn into getting the process over with as quickly as possible, without recognising the importance of your decision. But it is worth reminding yourself quickly of how crucial it really is for everyone involved.

▶ *Your organisation:* **When you buy a house, you have to pay for stamp duty, removals, change-of-address cards, and all the rest of it. It's an expensive exercise, even before you launch into the cost of keeping and**

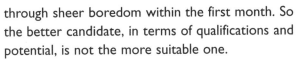

You want the most *suitable* candidate – not necessarily the best-qualified or the most experienced

SQUARE PEG ...

Have you ever worked with someone who was clearly in the wrong job? Remember what it was like – for you, for them, and for everyone else. Keep this in mind if you're tempted to rush through the process in a way that jeopardises your chances of appointing the most suitable candidate. We're going to do this fast, but we're not going to rush it.

maintaining the building. When your organisation recruits a new employee, they have to pay for advertising the post, mailing application forms (and the time it takes), organising and running the interviews (your time now, in other words), induction, and the ongoing cost of the employee. If you employ the wrong person, that's a lot of money down the drain.

▶ *Other team members:* If you appoint the wrong person to this post, how are their team mates going to feel? They are likely to be demoralised – their productivity may drop – and if you have to let an unsuitable new employee go, it's even more damaging.

▶ *The employee:* Suppose you appoint someone who moves to the area to take the job. Or who gives up a job with good prospects for this post. Or who is close to retirement and unlikely to find another job if this one falls through. Quite apart from the short-term demoralisation and

frustration, you may be doing someone long-term harm by offering them a job for which they aren't really suitable. If you could have identified this fact but didn't, you're carrying a big responsibility.

So that's why we're going to do this selection stuff properly. We're going to take any shortcuts we can, but not if they increase the risk of appointing the wrong candidate.

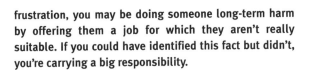

for next time

We're going to do this properly, but it's going to mean some hard work. Another time, you'll be doing yourself a big favour if you block in sacrosanct time in your diary for this process. Not just for the interviews, but also for:

▸ preparing the job description and employee specification (see Chapter 2)
▸ going through the application forms to select candidates to interview (Chapter 3)
▸ preparing questions (Chapter 4).

We'll be looking at all these later on, but actually doing them is a lot less stressful if you've eased the time pressure by setting aside time when you first advertised the post.

2 the vital documents

Paperwork ... aargh! The clock's ticking away and you're supposed to be playing with bits of administrative paperwork? Yep, 'fraid so. But it doesn't have to take long. And you may be able to delegate parts of it (but not all of it – you need to be involved).

Let's be rational about this. You can't hope to appoint the most suitable person for the job if you don't know what the job is, can you? So you need a basic description of the job just to make it clear. And the candidates will need to see it too (in an ideal world you'd have sent it out with the application forms), so they can make certain that this is the job they want. So the job description is one of your two vital documents.

The other one is the employee specification. You must decide what sort of person you are looking for to fill this post. Do they need to be able to use certain types of software? Must they have an HGV licence? Should they be confident and friendly to deal with customers over the counter? This, together with the job description, gives you a full picture of the hypothetical person you are looking for. Then your job is simply to match the real candidate with this hypothetical one.

THE JOB DESCRIPTION

You must have seen plenty of job descriptions. They usually go on for two or three close-typed pages, detailing exactly what the employee has to do, from opening the morning post to the precise procedures for returning faulty items. Well, we don't want one of those. We haven't even got time to read it, let alone write it.

We only need the important bits – the bits that are relevant to choosing the right person to do the job. When you want to buy a house, you don't describe your ideal house to the estate agent down to the last detail. They don't need to know exactly what furniture you are planning to fit into it, or whether you prefer a high- or low-level cistern for the lavatory. They just want to know how many bedrooms, what sort of location, whether you want a garden and that sort of basic guidelines.

You can't appoint the most suitable person for the job if you don't know what the job is

NO RUBBER STAMP

If you are advertising an existing post, you presumably already have a job description for it. This may well provide a handy shortcut. But look through it and make sure it still describes the job as you want it to be. Perhaps this is a good opportunity to change some of the responsibilities that go with this job, or perhaps the previous incumbent never actually did half this stuff, and it shouldn't be down there at all. So never settle for simply digging out the old job description without reviewing it.

The same goes for the job description for this post you're advertising. It need only be an outline of the key facts about the job. It should give:

▶ **job title**

▶ **who they report to**

▶ **overall objective**

▶ **key responsibilities**

▶ **other information for the applicants.**

The easiest way to explain this fully is with an example. Let's suppose you're interviewing for a receptionist. The job description should look something like this:

JOB DESCRIPTION

Job title Receptionist

Reporting to Customer service manager

Overall objective To provide a telephone and face-to-face receptionist service for all callers and visitors to the building

Key responsibilities

1 Greet visitors in a friendly and helpful manner to give a good impression of the organisation, and notify staff promptly when visitors arrive

2 Answer the switchboard promptly in a friendly and helpful manner, and:

   Put calls through to the appropriate extension

   Take accurate messages and pass them on promptly

   Give information and help

3 Keep the reception area tidy

Further information

- Dynamic young company in central London office

- Training with a view to promotion within the company

- Childcare allowance available

Never settle for simply digging out the old job description without reviewing it

FROM THE HORSE'S MOUTH

If you're really pushed for time – or even if you're not – why not ask the person who is vacating the post to draft a list of key responsibilities that they feel describes the job they really do? Ask them to disregard what the old job description says (it may be very similar, or wildly different) and to come up with a short list. Then go through this yourself – properly – to check whether you want to change or add to it.

Of course, some jobs have more key responsibilities than others, but you shouldn't need to list more than half a dozen or so at most, and three or four often cover everything.

It should be clear that you need to go through this thought-process yourself, as it will help you enormously when you come to review the applications and interview the candidates. But you can always get someone else to type it up into a standard format.

THE EMPLOYEE SPECIFICATION

You've established what the job is now, but you still need to decide what kind of person you are looking for to fill it. When you look for a house, you have a whole list of requirements that are not part of the description you give the estate agent. You told them what job the house needs to do – it needs to provide four bedrooms and a small garden not far from the shops and the station. But in fact, of all the houses in town that can do this job, only some will suit you.

You have your own list. For a start, it needs to have a bedroom that will take your huge old bed you inherited from your grandmother. It needs a big dining room or family kitchen because you often hold large dinner parties. And the garden has to face the right way to grow your prize sunflowers. Ideally, you'd like a range cooker, too, although you could always put one in yourself.

In other words, you have a list of requirements – some essential and some simply desirable – that any house will need to fulfil. And the same goes for the new employee you take on. They must have certain skills and attributes, and you need to identify these in advance. Otherwise you may not recognise them when you see them. And, just like your ideal house, some of these will be essentials while others will simply be preferences. For example, if you have a lot of foreign visitors, you might consider it essential for your receptionist to speak French, and desirable for them also to speak Spanish.

The best, and fastest, way to draw up an employee specification is to draw a matrix:

	Skills	Attributes
Essential		
Desirable		

Now you simply fill in each box with the relevant skills or attributes that your hypothetical ideal employee should have. Anyone you consider must meet every requirement in the top two boxes. You will want to find someone who also meets many of the requirements in the two bottom boxes.

Again, there's no need – and no time – to write an essay here. You are probably looking for around three or four skills and half a dozen attributes altogether. These might include:

- ▶ *Skills:* qualifications, foreign languages, understanding of particular software programs, problem-solving skills, supervisory skills, book keeping.

- ▶ *Attributes:* good teamworker, ability to work to deadlines, flexibility, ability to think analytically, good eye for detail, good at communicating, able to work under pressure.

So let's see what your employee specification for that receptionist's job might look like:

	Skills	Attributes
Essential	▶ Experience in switchboard operation ▶ Fluent in French ▶ Helpful telephone manner and clear speaking voice	▶ Able to communicate with people at all levels ▶ Able to work under pressure ▶ Friendly and helpful manner
Desirable	▶ Some clerical experience	▶ Flexibility about working hours ▶ General neatness and tidiness ▶ Good attention to detail

Some attributes will be essentials while others will simply be preferences

DON'T GET PERSONAL

When it comes to personal attributes, make sure you remain objective. If a friendly and pleasant manner is necessary to the job – say, a receptionist – then include it in your employee specification. But don't put it in just because you think it would be nicer. It is unlikely to be a requirement for an in-house designer, for example.

There, that shouldn't have taken too long. But it should have given you a much clearer idea of what precisely you're looking for. You now have the two vital documents you need to tell you what the job is, and what kind of person will be suitable for it.

The job description should really be prepared well in advance, so that you can send it out with the application forms to anyone who requests one. It's only fair that applicants should know what the job they are applying for is. Don't send out an old, out-of-date job description that you haven't quite got round to updating – it could be extremely misleading.

The employee specification, although it should be drawn up in advance, is for your own information, however, and not for sending out to applicants.

When it comes to personal attributes, make sure you remain objective

3 sifting the applications

You may already have been through the application forms and shortlisted candidates for interview. In this case, you can skip on to the next chapter for now if you're pushed for time (but please come back and read this one next time you have a post to advertise). If you haven't yet been through this process, let's get cracking.

You have a pile of application forms in front of you, and you can't possibly interview all the applicants. You haven't got time to waste interviewing people who aren't suitable, and you don't want to waste their time either. So you need to sort these applications into two piles: those you want to interview and those you don't.

NARROWING THE FIELD

So just how are you going to narrow this pile down fast? It's simply a process of elimination. And how

> ### LOOK WITHIN
>
> It makes sense to fill vacancies internally if you can, so always give consideration to internal applicants. Not only do they already know your organisation, but the very fact that you consider them shows all your staff that you are positive about finding them opportunities for promotion. So you are benefiting the morale and the commitment of your workforce by encouraging internal applicants.

do you know what to eliminate? By using your job description and employee specification, that's how. See, they're coming in handy already.

Imagine that these applications are all the house details you've been sent by estate agents. They give you a photo of the front, a location, and measurements and details of each of the rooms, the garage, the garden and so on. If you're after a house, you can tell at a glance which are worth a visit and which aren't – you already know what requirements you gave the estate agents, and what else you need from any suitable house. If the information isn't comprehensive enough for you to be certain, you'll probably opt to take a look just in case. You're just doing the same thing now with job applications instead of house details.

So simply go through the applications and compare each one with your two vital documents. Weed out any applicants whose experience or attributes clearly don't fit these descriptions. Suppose your job description indicates that you need someone who must work closely as part of a team. An applicant who has always worked alone and shows no other team-working potential (such as listing formation parachuting under hobbies) is unlikely to be suitable.

Likewise, if your employee specification shows that you need someone with experience of operating a switchboard, applications from people without this experience are unlikely to be worth pursuing.

thinking smart

BE FLEXIBLE

Although you need to measure each application against your two vital documents, it is worth bearing in mind that the best candidate doesn't always fulfil the criteria exactly. If a particular application really impresses you despite one or two reservations, there's no law that says you can't interview the candidate anyway. Some skills or attributes may be essential, but don't be too rigid over everything, or your best applicant may never make it as far as the interviews.

As well as comparing the applications with your job description and employee specification, you also need to look for any other obvious omissions or suspect areas in each application. Probably the most common of these are:

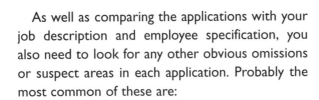 significant gaps between jobs with no obvious explanation

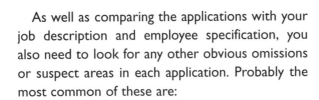 an applicant who has taken drops in salary, perhaps when changing jobs, again without any clear reason.

These factors prove nothing in themselves, but they are pointers to potential problems. Of course, employment gaps might be explained by illness, or taking breaks to have a family. A drop in salary might have been worth it for a more interesting job. On the other hand, the explanations might not be so innocent. In other words, if the application is otherwise impressive, you can still interview these applicants (and question them about these things, as we'll see later on).

But in general, gaps and salary drops add to the balance of points against, and may swing your judgement in favour of the 'no interview' pile. The important thing, of course, is to make sure that even though you're up against the clock, you still notice these kinds of omissions or areas of doubt.

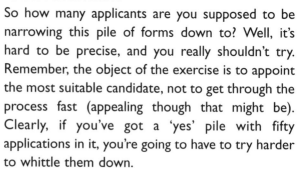

So how many applicants are you supposed to be narrowing this pile of forms down to? Well, it's hard to be precise, and you really shouldn't try. Remember, the object of the exercise is to appoint the most suitable candidate, not to get through the process fast (appealing though that might be). Clearly, if you've got a 'yes' pile with fifty applications in it, you're going to have to try harder to whittle them down.

But the real question is: how many promising applicants are there? If there are nine in your 'yes' pile, it's no good thinking that you'll have to get rid of one because there are only eight interview slots in the day. You might reject the one who would have been your best candidate. And anyway, you haven't got time to spend hours deliberating over which one should go. Just interview them all, and squeeze up the schedule or spend two long half-days interviewing instead.

Equally, if you have five applications that stand out, don't try to find three more just to fill up the day. You can't afford to waste that sort of time – and nor can they. So be as ruthless as you need to be to get the numbers down to a sensible level, and then interview everyone who meets these criteria.

WHAT ARE YOU AFTER?

If suitability for this post rests chiefly on experience and skills, it will probably be easy to reduce the list for interview to only a few candidates. When personality is more important, for instance for a receptionist's job, you'll need to see more of the applicants in order to decide who is most suitable.

THANKS BUT NO THANKS

What do you do about all those applicants you're not going to interview? No matter how busy you are, you must write to them as promptly as possible. Send them a polite note of thanks for their interest, but let them know that you won't be inviting them for an interview. If you don't have time, delegate the job but sign the letters yourself. Remember that these people may not be suitable for this post, but they may be ideal for another job with your organisation in the future. So make sure you leave them with a good impression of your friendliness and efficiency.

SETTING UP THE INTERVIEWS

When you invite candidates to interview, try to be as flexible as you can about times. It may be hard for

Get the numbers down to a sensible level, and then interview everyone who meets the criteria

them to get time off, especially if you've left things a little late. So give them as much leeway as you can.

When it comes to allocating time for interviews, don't imagine you can interview each candidate successfully in fifteen minutes (much as you might like to be able to). As a rule of thumb, allow about three-quarters of an hour for interviews for a junior post (plus another ten to fifteen to make notes and then refresh your mind about the next candidate). If you're interviewing for a senior management position, you might well need to allow about half a day for each applicant.

thinking smart

PICK UP THE PHONE

Always get someone to phone candidates to arrange interview times, rather than writing. It makes it much quicker to agree a time, and it ensures that promising applicants know you're interested as soon as possible – before they accept another post elsewhere.

If you have received a large proportion of applications from people who are not suitable for the job, something has gone wrong. Most of these people would probably never have applied if they had realised they had no chance. You can save yourself and them a lot of time by making it clear in the original recruitment ad, and in the information you send out with the application form, exactly what your requirements are. So another time make sure you write informative job advertisements, and send out the job description along with the application form.

Another option when time is less pressing is to pay an agency to find you a shortlist of candidates. Ironically, although this will actually save you time, you need to get the ball rolling earlier than this. You'll still have to produce a job description and employee specification, show the agency around and brief them fully. But they will then take care of the advertising, sending out application forms and going through the replies, before giving you your interview list.

The unsuccessful applicants may be ideal for another job with your organisation in the future

4 the questions

I know you haven't got time to waste preparing these interviews, but you're going to look a fool if you go in there and don't know what you want to ask. Equally, you'll look pretty stupid if it turns out when your new appointee arrives on their first day that they've never operated a switchboard, but you forgot to check that one out.

So planning your questions is a necessity, not a luxury. That said, you don't need a detailed list of fifty questions for each applicant. You need two sets of questions:

1 questions that you ask all the applicants

2 specific questions for each applicant.

If you design your questions well, you don't need that many of them. There's nothing wrong with letting the conversation flow, and asking questions that crop up as you go along as well as those on your prepared list.

GENERAL QUESTIONS

When you're looking for a house, you want to check certain things about all of them: have they got off-road parking for two cars? Do they have central heating? Are the fixtures and fittings included in the price?

The general questions, which you will want to ask all the applicants, are the key questions arising from the job description and the employee specification. You will want to find out how their experience relates to the job description, details of their qualifications, skills and work history, and their approach to customer care, corporate change, or integrated IT systems, or whatever is relevant to this particular job.

thinking smart

FEWER AND BETTER

The more open the questions you ask, the better. For one thing, you will need to prepare fewer questions, and for another you will get fuller answers. So instead of asking 'What switchboards have you operated?' try asking 'Tell me about the switchboards you've operated in the past.' Instead of their simply listing them, this encourages the interviewee to say which were easy or difficult, how much experience they have of each, and so on. With one question, you've found out plenty of detail.

So assemble a list of broad questions to get them to discuss these things. For example:

- **'This job involves dealing with customers face-to-face and on the phone. What do you think are the most important aspects of good customer care?'**
- **'What experience do you have of handling customers?'**
- **'Tell me about your experience of working under pressure.'**

You'll probably find that you need only devise half a dozen or so of these broad, open questions – which won't take you too long. And you can follow any interesting threads in the answer on an *ad hoc* basis. But it is important to ask everyone the same core questions so that you can assess each candidate on the same basis.

INDIVIDUAL QUESTIONS

You will also have individual questions for the applicants. Again, to follow the analogy of buying a house, these are like the questions you identified from the individual house details. For example: is the heating oil, gas or electric? Could the third bedroom be converted into another bathroom easily? Does the garage have a connecting door to the kitchen, or is the only access external?

You don't have to spend ages drawing up neat lists here – just annotate each application form or stick a

PAST, PRESENT AND FUTURE

Aim to ask each candidate individual questions about their past experience, their present attitudes and circumstances, and their future ambitions. This will give you a broad picture of the applicant by the end of the interview.

Ask everyone the same core questions so that you can assess each candidate on the same basis

post-it note on it (as long as it won't come adrift). You're simply drawing your attention to the points you want to raise. Yes, this means you're going to have to go through the application forms individually, but if you do this soon after the shortlisting process you'll probably remember most of the significant points from each application anyway (now there's one of the few real advantages of cutting the preparation fine).

You might make a note to ask about:

- ▶ a gap in employment

- ▶ a career change

- ▶ their reason for leaving previous jobs

- ▶ their style of working

- ▶ the fact that they appear overqualified for the post

- ▶ a useful-looking skill, such as fluency in a foreign language

CAREFUL WORDING

Generally, you don't need to design the individual questions exactly, but simply to note down the points to cover. However, if you want to raise a delicate topic that you think might be hard to bring up, it is wise to plan the precise wording of the question in advance to make it easy on yourself.

▶ **a particular hobby that indicates a relevant attribute (such as determination, or a fondness for working alone).**

These are only a few examples – there are many possibilities. The point is to make sure that you touch on any subject that you think is particularly relevant, whether positive or negative.

WHO'S ASKING THE QUESTIONS?

There's just one more thing. At the end of the interview, you should ask each candidate if they have any questions for you. When they do, it's going to look a whole lot better if you know the answers. So prepare yourself for this by anticipating any likely questions. For a start, you should arm yourself with a copy of your terms and conditions of employment. In addition, you should know the answers to questions about:

- salary
- working hours
- holiday entitlement
- what training you will give the successful candidate
- career prospects
- how you will notify candidates
- whether you will hold second interviews.

and any other topics you think are likely to be raised.

The process of planning the questions really doesn't have to be a long one at all. But it is an essential one if you want to be sure of appointing the right candidate.

for next time

It is well worth talking through your list of general questions with your boss or a colleague, to make sure you've covered the essentials. By the same token, it can help to ask someone else to look through the applications individually for you to identify any areas that are worth going into more detail.

5 setting the scene

You're almost there. You've written your job description and employee specification, you've been through the applications, and you've prepared two lists of questions: one general list for everyone, and a brief list of questions or notes for each applicant individually. You're doing well, and it shouldn't have taken you too long to get here. This chapter is about the last few loose ends to tie up before the candidates arrive for their interviews.

The crucial thing to remember about selection is that it is a two-way process. I'm sure you remember what it's like looking for a job yourself. You are invited to several interviews and (you hope) offered more than one position. So you get to choose which organisation you would like to work for out of two or three, if you're lucky.

Your best candidate will have applied for other posts, and may well be someone else's best

DON'T BE CLEVER

You've probably heard of all sorts of techniques to intimidate candidates, ruses for challenging them, and questions for baffling them. Once in a blue moon there might be a valid and justifiable reason for employing these techniques. But for the vast majority of posts it isn't a clever approach. It's far better to be pleasant and friendly, and to put the interviewee at their ease.

Selection is a two-way process

candidate too. So when they come to select which job they prefer to take, how will you ensure they accept your offer? This chapter is all about treating the candidates in a way that will make them feel that yours is the organisation – and you are the boss – they would most like to work for. Much of it is also plain courtesy, but it can make the difference between whether or not you get the candidate you want.

PREPARE THE ROOM

The traditional image of an interview has the candidate sitting across a desk from the interviewer. But in fact this is a very formal, intimidating set-up for an interview. It is far better to remove this psychological barrier, and seat both yourself and the interviewee (and anyone else present) in comfortable chairs. This will encourage the interviewee to relax and open up.

If your office can't accommodate this kind of relaxed seating, try to borrow another room that is more suitable. If you really can't even do this, at least move the chairs away from the desk.

MAKE THEM FEEL IMPORTANT

There are plenty of other small but important measures you can take to make each candidate feel that you value them. For a start, make sure that you are not the only one prepared for this interview: check that reception has a list of names and interview times, along with anyone who is showing them into the interview room.

- **Each candidate should be welcomed by someone – even if it's the receptionist – as soon as they arrive so that they know they are expected. The receptionist should treat them with the same importance as they would a member of the board or an important customer.**

- **Forestall any interruptions. Divert calls and close the office door, with a notice on it if necessary to ensure that the interviewee has your full attention and knows it.**

- **Start the interview promptly. It is disrespectful to keep people waiting.**

FIRST IMPRESSIONS

When the interviewee enters the room, you should stand up, smile, shake hands and address them by name. Tell them who you are, and invite them to sit down.

Make each candidate feel that you value them

▶ **Have the job description, employee specification and the candidate's application form to hand during the interview, to show you've done your homework and are treating this interview with the importance it deserves.**

HELP THEM RELAX

Here are a few more steps you can take to help interviewees to calm down if they are nervous, and to prepare themselves for the interview. Remember, this could be a deeply important time for them; they may really want this job.

▶ **Make sure someone offers to take their coat, and show them to the toilet if they want to visit it.**

▶ **Offer them a cup of coffee or tea, or a glass of water, either before or during the interview.**

▶ **Leave copies of the annual report or company newsletter in the waiting area for candidates to look at, and make sure the waiting area – whether it is reception or a corner of an office – is clean and comfortable.**

- Make sure there is a mirror they can use somewhere in the waiting area.

- If you want to keep tabs on the time, don't unsettle the candidate by looking at your watch constantly. Make sure there's a clock you can look at easily.

thinking smart

BREAKING THE ICE

If you sense that the candidate is nervous, try to put them at their ease for a minute or two before you start the interview proper. Find something to chat about informally on their application form. For example, 'I see you trained in Manchester. I used to work there. What did you think of the city?' Not only will it help them relax, it also proves you've read the application form.

for next time

Give yourself time to arrange a suitable room to hold the interviews in, and make sure every candidate has been given a time and date for the interview in writing, along with directions for getting to you, several days ahead of the interview.

If you sense that the candidate is nervous, try to put them at their ease for a minute or two before you start the interview proper

6 the interview

So here you are. All the preparation is done and you're ready to start the interviews themselves. You should have four pieces of paper with you for each interview:

▶ **the job description**

▶ **the employee specification**

▶ **the application form, with notes of questions arising from it**

▶ **your list of general questions that you are asking all the candidates.**

The room is set up comfortably and reception (and anyone else who needs to know) is expecting the candidates, so it's time to get cracking on the first interview.

This book is about how to think fast and get through the job as quickly as possible. However, you

thinking smart

NO SECOND CHANCE

Except for the most high-powered posts, second interviews should only be necessary if you are shortlisting candidates for someone else (together with you or not) to interview later. A second interview is not just an opportunity for you to have another go at spotting the most suitable candidate. You don't have that sort of time to waste. So do the job properly first time, and you won't need a second attempt.

cannot rush an interview. What you can do, however, is to conduct it so effectively that you cover everything you need to, and ensure that your techniques will show up the best candidate first time. That way, you won't have to waste time on second interviews or, worse, appoint the wrong candidate.

When you're looking for your dream house, your best bet is to allow plenty of time to look at each house in detail. You wouldn't rush a viewing. Then the odds are you won't need another look to make up your mind – unless you need someone else to see the house too.

THE INTERVIEW STRUCTURE

Broadly speaking, you should always follow the same structure for an interview:

1 Welcome the candidate and put them at their ease.

2 Ask the questions from your general list, i.e. those arising from the job specification.

3 Ask the questions you identified from the application form, i.e. those that are specific to the candidate.

4 Invite the candidate to ask you any questions he or she has.

Depending on how much time you have, you can pace yourself according to this structure so that you don't get behind schedule. You need allow only a minute or two for the opening courtesies, and about five minutes for the candidate's questions (and for you to tell them what happens next and thank them for coming). Apart from that you can roughly halve the remaining time, using the first half to ask them your general questions, and the second half to ask individual questions.

THE TECHNIQUES

Interviewing is not as simple as just firing off a list of questions. There are techniques you need to use to draw out the candidate, and to get them to give you honest and illuminating answers. And the two key techniques – which go together – are listening and encouraging the candidate to talk.

Let's start with listening. It may sound like an obvious skill, but many managers fail to do it when interviewing (a lot of them fail to do it the rest of the time as well). However, if you don't listen well you will miss vital clues, as well as possibly unsettling your interviewee.

There's more to listening than you might think. Listening properly means taking it all in, not just hearing what the other person says. You know yourself that you can tell when someone is really listening to you and when they aren't; what you may not realise is *how* you can tell. It's something we sense unconsciously as a rule, but there are signs that show the other person you're listening. More importantly, the signs mean you *are* listening, so you won't miss a trick in the interview.

So what are these signs? Well, here are the key ones:

- ▶ **Make frequent eye contact with the interviewee.**
- ▶ **Look interested and show that your attention is on them – don't keep checking the time or getting absorbed in your papers.**
- ▶ **Make the occasional one- or two-word note if you wish, but don't spend the whole time writing while they are**

talking (don't worry: we'll sort out time for taking notes later).

- Make listening noises from time to time, such as 'uh-huh' and 'hmmm'.

- Don't interrupt them while they're speaking.

- Repeat key points back to them occasionally to show you were listening. For example, 'So you'd planned to go into engineering from the start? That's very dedicated.'

It's easier than it sounds: these are both the symptoms and the causes of listening. Do them, and you'll find you're listening. Listen naturally, and you'll find you do all these things instinctively.

The second key technique is encouraging the candidate to talk. With some, of course, this is no problem. In some cases, getting them to *stop* talking is more of a challenge (especially if they are nervous). But many people clam up in interviews,

thinking smart

BODY LANGUAGE

The way you sit helps to show you are listening – and the right posture will make it easier for you to listen. Sit in a relaxed position, but lean forward slightly to show you're being attentive. If you cross everything – arms and legs – you will appear defensive, which makes it harder for your interviewee to talk freely. So go for a reasonably open posture.

especially at the start. If you put them at their ease and listen well, they should open up quite quickly. However, there are plenty of ways of getting them talking almost from the start.

Start with the past

People find it much easier to talk about their past than about, say, their attitudes or their ambitions. It is safe ground, and they don't have to think too hard. So it's an easy place to begin. Ask them about their education or their early career, and watch them relax as they talk.

Let them do the talking

You want the interviewee to do about seventy-five to eighty per cent of the talking in the interview. If

thinking smart

PAST, PRESENT AND FUTURE

You could break down the first main part of the interview – the general questions for everybody – into a series of questions that goes through each candidate's career from a suitable starting point (school for a candidate in their early twenties, but maybe early career for a fifty-year-old). Talk about their past, then their present job, attitudes, approaches to work and so on, and then their future ambitions.

you tell them too much about the job, they'll adapt their answers to suit what they think you want. You want to hear about them, so ask the questions and then let them get on with it, while you simply steer them in the right direction. You'll do most of your talking in the opening welcome, and in the last few minutes when they get to ask you questions.

Ask open questions

A shy or nervous candidate may well restrict themselves to brief answers to your questions if they can. So make sure they can't. Don't ask them closed questions – ones to which they can answer 'yes', 'no', 'twelve' or 'green with red stripes'. Ask open questions, to which they have to give a full answer. Open questions tend to start with 'how', 'what' or 'why'. For example: 'How did you come to choose research as a career?' or 'What made you apply for this post?' Another useful phrase at interview is 'Tell me about … your interests at school / your ideas on how businesses can integrate more fully with the Internet / your long-term career objectives', and so on.

Empathise

The candidate may be doing most of the talking, but you're interjecting to ask them questions. You

TAKING THE WHEEL

You're in charge of this interview. So it's up to you to keep garrulous candidates under control. You have to keep these interviews running on time. The best technique is this: take over the wheel; don't try to stand in front of the car. In other words, don't block them, just steer them on to the right subject. Find a link and use it. If they're talking at length about how good their university course was, you might say: 'That's what got you interested in a career in marketing, then? So how did you get your first job once you'd got your degree?'

can help to encourage interviewees to talk by showing you're on their side, and want to hear more. So, as you go from one answer to the next question, be human and inject a little friendliness. For example, if you've just asked them what their least favourite subject at school was, you might say, 'I never got on too well with history either. Why do you think it was your least favourite?' You can throw in any comment that is honest and friendly, to make the encounter more natural, from 'That's an interesting answer' to 'I'm impressed. Nothing would induce *me* to jump out of an aeroplane at several thousand feet.'

STAY ON TOP

Just as some candidates clam up, others try to take control of the interview, and talk about what they want to say, not what you want to hear. Don't stand for it: it's your interview and you should be in control. A simple technique is to start asking a few closed questions. If open questions get people to open up, closed questions get them to close down. You can bring the interview back on to your territory by asking closed questions such as, 'How many years have you been in your present job?' or 'Do you have a driving licence?'

DON'T HAVE OPINIONS

You know perfectly well that if you tell an estate agent that you're looking for a house with excellent views, they'll assure you the house they've just sent you details about has the kind of views you only dream of. Interviewees are much the same. If you tell them you think the latest legislation affecting your industry stinks, and then ask them what they think about it, what do you suppose their answer will be?

Yet many managers do precisely this. It may not be as obvious as this example, but they give away their attitudes before asking the interviewee for theirs. And of course any smart candidate will tell you what you want to hear. It can be hard to catch yourself leading the candidate to the answer you want to hear. You might, for example, say: 'I think the Internet is one of the most exciting developments of the last few years. Tell me what experience you've had with it, and how you feel about it.' Even this signposts the type of answer you want to hear.

This really can be tough, because it's the way we often talk to our colleagues and friends. But you're not having a cosy chat now, or even a business debate. You're interviewing, and that is something quite different.

DIGGING DEEPER

This all sounds very nice and friendly so far, and so it should. But things aren't always so easy.

thinking smart

ELEMENTARY, MY DEAR WATSON

Try imagining yourself as one of your favourite detectives – Morse, Sherlock Holmes or Poirot – interviewing a witness to try to get at the truth (you'd be well advised to think of the candidate as a witness rather than a suspect). You're looking for clues, and giving away nothing in case it muddies the evidence. This approach may help you to keep your own views hidden during the interview.

Sometimes there are delicate topics that you want to introduce – touchy areas, perhaps, where you're not sure how the interviewee will feel about the question. Perhaps you want to know why they changed career to what appears to be a less challenging and lower-powered job. Maybe you want to know why they haven't had a promotion in nine years with the same company.

We get very sensitive where other people are concerned – understandably. But think about your house-hunting for a moment. If the owners are showing you around a house and you notice a patch of discoloured wallpaper, do you maintain a polite silence? Of course you don't. You say, 'Is that a patch of damp there?' You're not going to risk spending all that money on a house that turns out to have a damp problem you hadn't budgeted for.

Well, you're about to spend as much money on a new employee, so you're going to have to adopt the same approach to any areas of concern: ask about them. And the technique is blindingly simple. You don't faff about, embroider the question or sound embarrassed. You simply ask.

▶ **What made you choose this career change?**

▶ **Have you applied for promotion while you've been with your present employer?**

- ⏵ **What were you doing during the year between these two jobs?**

- ⏵ **Why did you take a job that entailed a salary drop when you left Zedcon?**

Simple, huh?

The thing is, you *have* to ask these questions. Otherwise you can't find out whether the candidate is suitable for the job. They may look terrific on paper, but that one-year gap could be concealing a recent spell drying out from alcoholism – not ideal if the job involves entertaining a lot of corporate clients.

Equally, you may be tempted to reject them because of that suspicious-looking gap when a little

thinking smart

AN AIR OF AUTHORITY

It is much easier to keep the interview on course, and ask the questions you need to, if you have the air of being in charge. This doesn't mean dominating or bullying – far from it. It simply means coming across as confident and sure of yourself, and knowing what you're doing (this is one of the many reasons why the preparation was worth it). If you behave confidently from the outset – standing up, offering a hand to shake, and greeting the candidate with assurance – they will accept your authority without question.

questioning would establish that they were taking time out to look after a dying relative. So you must investigate these areas for both your sakes.

What is more, any candidates worth their salt will be expecting you to ask them this sort of question, so they are unlikely to be offended by it. So long as you're not personal or rude in your questioning, but simply ask the question straight, they have no reason even to be surprised, let alone put out. Would you be?

Suppose, as sometimes happens, you get an answer to your tricky question that doesn't really satisfy you. What do you do then? The answer here is that you must keep asking the question: 'I'm still not clear why this job you took after Zedcon was worth a salary drop for you?'

And if this still doesn't get an answer that satisfies you (one way or the other), you can simply express your doubts squarely. Say what's bothering you. And, once again, tell it how it is. For example: 'Can I tell you what's worrying me? We're looking for someone with drive and ambition. The successful candidate is likely to find themselves well on their way up the career ladder here in a few years' time. You've been doing the same job at Zedcon for nine years now, and I have to ask myself whether you really have the ambition to take this job where we expect it to go.'

CUTTING BOTH WAYS

Remember that selection is a two-way process. The candidate may have reservations about working for you which you want to set at rest. So probe and ask questions at the end of the interview to make sure they have no lingering doubts. If you suspect they do, put it to them straight: 'I wouldn't want you to leave with any unanswered questions. Please feel free to ask if anything is bothering you. I sense you may have misgivings about our training?'

This gives the candidate an opportunity to put their case. Maybe the job at Zedcon has been expanding and growing, and, although the job title hasn't changed, the responsibilities and the expertise needed to do it have grown beyond measure in the last nine years. Then again, maybe this candidate just has no personal drive. Whichever is the case, you won't know unless you explain the problem.

THE LEGAL POSITION

There are laws governing what you can and can't ask candidates at interview. These can vary, but the object is to make sure that all job applicants are treated fairly and without discrimination. You will need to talk to your legal or HR department if you want detailed advice, but broadly speaking you cannot turn down an applicant for discriminatory reasons – and quite right too, of course.

If you reject a candidate who might be subject to unlawful discrimination, you must be able to demonstrate that you had some other, legitimate reason for turning them down. This means that it is very unwise to try to elicit any information you don't need, especially if it could be seen as discriminatory. For example, don't ask a woman if she is planning to start a family – an affirmative answer could be seen as a reason not to take her on, even if you in fact turn her down for some other reason altogether.

This whole legal area can seem like a minefield, but it doesn't need to be. As a basic guideline, if you have a sound business reason for asking a question, that's fine. If you don't, why are you wasting time asking it? If you want a checklist of topics to avoid unless you have a good reason to investigate them, here's a rough (but not exhaustive) guide:

- ▶ **colour, race, religion, nationality**
- ▶ **age (except to ask if they are over eighteen)**
- ▶ **sex**

- ▶ disability, handicap, medical history
- ▶ marital status, maiden name, details of children, childcare arrangements, future plans for a family
- ▶ height and weight
- ▶ history of any compensation claims against a previous employer
- ▶ English-language skills
- ▶ details of arrests or spent convictions, or military service discharge
- ▶ credit rating or history of bankruptcy.

CLOSING THE INTERVIEW

Once you have asked everything you need to, and your time is almost up, ask the candidate if they have any questions for you. Give them time to answer this question, and tell them anything you think they might need to know that hasn't been mentioned yet – from the fact that you have a crèche to the training programme you're offering.

Finish the interview by signalling clearly that the end has come, and letting the interviewee know what will happen next: 'We'll be in touch at the beginning of next week.' Thank them for coming, explain any arrangements for claiming travel expenses, and tell them how to find their way out. Ideally you should post someone to show them out, find them their coat or whatever. Otherwise they may feel that now you've finished with them nobody's bothered any more. So look after them all the way back to the front door.

for next time

Make a note of the questions candidates ask you at interview, and make sure next time that you're ready with all the answers. Every time you conduct interviews you discover a little more about what the candidates want to know about your organisation. This means that you can be that little bit more prepared each time you run interviews than you were the last time.

fast thinking pause

Time for a break, we're nearly there.

Look after them all the way back to the front door

7 decision time

Well, that's it. You've seen all the candidates and it's time to make a decision. What's more, you haven't got time to dither over it for hours or delay it for weeks. You've got to get on with it. But it has to be the right decision, too.

And it's never easy, of course. One of your interviewees may have come across as a confident and friendly personality for the receptionist job, but another was much more experienced in switchboard operating. And then there was the one who just seemed to have a natural rapport with people, but had never done any reception work at all. It is rarely obvious who the most suitable candidate is.

YOUR NOTES

But there is one thing that will help you make your decision. Your notes. You remember: the ones I told you not to take during the interview. Well, you can't take them during it, but you can make notes immediately afterwards, as soon as the candidate has left the room. And you must. It's amazing what you can forget after half a dozen or so interviewees have passed before your eyes.

These notes don't have to take long, but they are crucial. They will be your basis for the final decision on whom to appoint. So give them the attention they deserve. Allow yourself about ten minutes between interviews for making notes.

thfhihthinkingtsmart

FINDING A BALANCE

Whatever your system, you'll want to see who has scored best or been given the best notes out of all the candidates. This is generally the most suitable candidate. However, it doesn't have to be, especially if two or more candidates are running neck and neck. The notes and scores count for a lot, but don't disregard your own gut feelings. Take them into account; it's possible they may swing the balance in the end.

It is rarely obvious who the most suitable candidate is

One of the most effective ways to take notes is to have a sheet of paper for each candidate, with headings on it such as 'experience', 'qualifications', 'attitude', 'technical knowledge', 'skills' and so on – whatever is relevant to this post. Then you can simply jot down key points under each heading.

You might also like to have a combined 'score sheet' for all the candidates. The candidates' names go down the side, and there are columns headed 'skills', 'experience', 'attitude' and so on. Give each candidate a score out of ten in each column. If some factors are more important than others, you can weight the scoring in their favour by marking these columns out of twenty. Fill in each candidate's row of marks as soon as their interview is over. At the end, you can see who has scored the most marks:

	Skills /20	Qualifications /10	Experience /20	Technical knowledge /10	Attitude /10	Total /70
Candidate A	15	8	10	10	9	52
Candidate B	14	7	15	7	8	51
Candidate C	12	7	16	6	6	47
Candidate D	12	6	15	5	6	44

This is a useful approach, but you shouldn't rely on it totally. In the example above, you'll notice

THE RIGHT CRITERIA

One of the key things to bear in mind when you are making your choice is that you must measure each candidate individually against the standards for the job. You are not measuring them against each other. A scoresheet, while not a final decider, can help you to look at the candidates in the light of the criteria you set at the start of the process (when you drew up the job description and the employee specification).

that candidate A has the highest score. However, look at the 'experience' column. This candidate is far less experienced than the others. You might decide that this is acceptable, in view of the outstanding performance otherwise. On the other hand you might decide that it still rules them out for the post, given that there is another promising candidate only one point behind on the scoresheet.

So those are your notes. There's no need for long essays; you just need to record enough information to help you make the right choice.

BACKING UP YOUR DECISION

You may be a naturally cautious decision-maker, in which case you will no doubt want to do whatever you can to be sure that your choice of candidate is

There is one thing that will help you make your decision: your notes

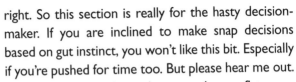

right. So this section is really for the hasty decision-maker. If you are inclined to make snap decisions based on gut instinct, you won't like this bit. Especially if you're pushed for time too. But please hear me out.

The odds are that when you buy a flat or a house, however sure you are that it's right, you'll still get a survey and do a search on the property. For the money you'll be spending, you'd be daft not to. And you may be a fast thinker, but you're not stupid. When it comes to checking references and possibly even qualifications, these are simply the employment equivalents of doing a survey and a search. You're about to commit as much money as you would on a new house (the only difference being that it's not your own money – but that argument isn't going to impress your boss).

In the worst cases, the most successful bluffers are very often the most impressive candidates. After all, if you have no compunction about stretching the truth, you can make yourself sound pretty good, and such candidates tend to be brimming with confidence and self-assurance. More realistically, many candidates will not be hardened fraudsters, but they will obviously paint the best picture of themselves that they can. If they are naturally confident and personable, they will come across well even if their record isn't quite so ideal.

THE MISSING LINK

The most obvious references for anyone to give are their current employer and their previous one. But people don't tend to give references they don't think will speak well of them. Many people leave their current employer off their references because they don't want them to know they're looking for a new job. But if the previous employer is also missing, it should make you wonder why. The best bet is to ask the candidate straight during the interview: 'Can you tell me why your references don't include either your present employer or your last one?' There may be a good reason, of course, but you won't find out unless you ask.

References

So when you think you know who you want to appoint, check their references first. It's always best to do this by phone, since people speak more freely than they write – they may not want a permanent record of their comments, for legal reasons apart from anything else.

Even on the phone, you're not likely to get any blatant negative comments from referees; they will probably be quite subtle in their hints. Apart from anything else, the law of slander applies to telephone references, and they will probably know

Checking references is simply the employment equivalent of doing a survey on a house

ONE MAN'S MEAT...

The fact that a past employer has a negative comment about your candidate isn't necessarily a bad thing. It depends on your requirements for the job. Suppose two referees mention that your candidate isn't at their best under pressure. Does this actually matter to you? Some negative comments may even signal positive benefits to you. A comment such as 'He doesn't like having to stick to the rules' may be the sign you want if you're looking for someone who can employ initiative and work off their own back (so long as they're not going to lock all the fire doors, of course, or bring a loaded gun into the office).

this. So what they *don't* say may be as telling as what they do. You can, of course, ask specific questions, but there's no point trying to pressure a referee into answering a question they don't want to.

A referee's opinion is, of course, only one view, and as such it shouldn't influence you too heavily (unless they tell you something really terrible, such as that the candidate you're interviewing for the post of minibus driver was sacked for being drunk while driving a company vehicle; and how often is that likely to happen?). It is also possible that the referee wasn't a big fan of the candidate, so a single weak reference doesn't have to sway your view.

So what's the point of taking up references in that case? Well, what you're really looking for are any comments that reinforce your own reservations. If you suspect that this promising candidate may not work well under pressure, you should take note if a referee suggests this is the case (assuming it is important they should cope well). Obviously, if you talk to two or three referees and they all say the same thing, this too will start to give a more reliable picture.

Qualifications

Managers almost never check qualifications, and you may decide it isn't necessary. However, some people do claim qualifications they don't have in order to help clinch a job. And even if the qualification itself isn't that important to you, the fact that this person is prepared to lie about it might well sway your judgement of them. So check qualifications if you feel any kind of suspicion that they may not be genuine.

You should also check any qualification if it's essential, for example legal qualifications for a company lawyer. You should check them even if you feel no doubt that they are genuine. It's the only way to be cast-iron certain.

PASS IT ON

Checking qualifications is simply a matter of phoning the college, university or training provider concerned and asking them to confirm the qualification for you. So if time is at a premium, get someone else to do this for you.

Tests

There are loads of psychometric, intelligence and aptitude tests around that some organisations like to use. Don't do them just for fun; use these tests only if you really feel they can shed valuable light on whom you should appoint. Bear in mind that all these tests have limitations and can fail to spot certain strong positive or negative qualities or abilities that fall outside their scope. So use them as an additional resource to feed into your decision, but don't rely heavily on them.

As a general guideline, run the tests on all the candidates before the interviews if you wish, but don't look at the results until after the interviews, and after you have written notes and filled in the scoresheet if you're using one. This means you will use the test results only as a back-up to check your own conclusions – a much more sensible approach.

CUT YOUR LOSSES

Almost without exception (the exception being aptitude tests related directly to the post), you might as well abandon doing any tests if time is short, whatever your usual company practice is. The value they contribute just doesn't justify the time and cost of running them.

OTHER CONSIDERATIONS

There are two other factors in particular that you may need to consider in making your decision. The first of these is the danger of making moral judgements about candidates. We're all guilty of making such judgements at times. Maybe we think people ought to show plenty of application and the ability to stick at things. Perhaps we think a strong imagination is better than a poor one. Maybe we feel it is better for people to have some drive and ambition, or that being very shy is a real handicap.

In fact, these are all judgements and many of them are ill-advised. It may be better for *you* to be a certain way, and you may prefer the company of people who are like this. But different jobs have different requirements. There is, for example, a popular belief that it's a good thing to be a team player. But if you want someone to work as a designer, spending all day alone in the graphics studio, a real team player is the last person you need. They would be frustrated and lonely, and would probably leave before long for a job in a more sociable environment. So avoid making subjective judgements of this kind.

Fitting into a team

The other factor to consider is the question of who your new employee will be working with. If you're selecting someone to work as part of a close-knit project team, you'll need to take into account how each promising interviewee would mesh with the rest of the team.

thinking smart

MEET AND GREET

You can always get the team – or key players in it – to meet each candidate informally. Get the team leader to greet each candidate at reception and look after them until the interview starts. Or call the candidates in fifteen minutes early so they can have a chat over coffee with the rest of the team. This is only an informal meeting, but it makes the team feel involved, and they can tell you if they found anyone particularly promising or if there was a candidate they really didn't warm to.

Clearly, personality is a factor in who will fit into an existing team. If the team works well at the moment, it shouldn't be hard to find someone who can slot in easily. If things are a little strained, perhaps you will want to look for a natural diplomat, or someone who isn't likely to try to take over. Maybe the team needs someone laid-back, could do with a bit of an injection of energy, or would benefit from someone with a good sense of humour.

But you also need to take into account the team's natural abilities. Some people are naturally good at coming up with ideas, or at problem-solving, getting on with the hard graft, or encouraging co-operation from outside the team. You need to take these factors into account and find someone who will expand the abilities of the team as a unit. For example, if all the team are great at generating ideas, but not so strong on carrying them through, it might not be wise to appoint yet another ideas person, even if they have all the right qualifications and experience.

LETTING EVERYONE KNOW

Make your decision as promptly as you can, for everyone's sake. Once you have all the information, from the application forms to your own interview

TEAM ROLES AT WORK

When you have a little time, it's worth studying Dr Meredith Belbin's work on team roles. Start by looking at his book *Management Teams: Why they succeed or fail*, published by Butterworth-Heinemann. This will tell you all about the key roles you need to fill to create an effective team.

notes and any references, there's nothing to be gained by prevaricating. Don't rush the decision, but don't put it off either. If you find decision-making difficult (and plenty of managers do), you can always read *Fast Thinking: Decision*, also in this series.

If you're pushed for time, offer the job to your preferred candidate by phone (although a letter is just as good when time allows). You'll need to follow up the call with a letter in due course. Don't reject the next two candidates until you have a definite acceptance from your first choice.

Write as promptly as possible to all the other candidates, thanking them for their time and wishing them success in finding a position. Remember that they may be – or may talk to – potential future employees or customers, so you want to leave them with a warm impression of your organisation.

WHAT IF YOU DRAW A BLANK?

Sometimes, there simply isn't a suitable applicant to give the job to. No one really satisfies you that they can do the job well. So what then? The answer, I'm afraid, is that you have to go through the whole process again (stop groaning). The thing is, if you give the job to someone unsuitable:

Don't rush the decision, but don't put it off either

▶ **They won't do the job as well as you'd like, and they'll probably leave before long – at which point you'll have to go through it all again anyway.**

▶ **It's not fair on them, since they won't be happy and they won't do as well as they could in a more suitable job. And that could hold back their career.**

Before you repeat the exercise exactly, however, it would be smart to ask yourself why it didn't work this time. If you simply do the same thing again, why should you be any more successful? It may be that your requirements are unrealistic. Perhaps you're looking for a very experienced receptionist with a lot of peripheral skills, at a salary that no experienced receptionist would accept. Maybe you should raise the salary – or lower your requirements. Or perhaps you're trying to find someone with a huge range of skills to do a very pressured job. It might be better to split it into two jobs, each calling for a somewhat narrower range of skills.

CHANGE YOUR ADVERTISING

Your inability to find someone suitable this time may not be down to the nature of the job you're offering. Maybe you just haven't caught the eye of the most likely applicants. Perhaps you should advertise elsewhere – nationally instead of locally, or in trade publications, or to graduates. Or maybe you should look harder for suitable internal applicants. Perhaps the right person is out there somewhere … but you haven't found each other yet.

Most managers panic at the thought of not appointing someone, even if they're not ideal. After all, you've got to have a receptionist. It's no good putting up a sign for visitors saying, 'Sort yourselves out. We can't find a suitable receptionist. The coffee machine's over there.'

But think smart. There's always a better way than appointing the wrong person. You could delay your present receptionist's promotion, or ask them to stay beyond their period of notice. You could hire someone on a short-term contract. You could get a temp in. You could get everyone in the sales office to cover for an hour a day. You could move someone over from another department for a few weeks. You could get your calls routed through an external switchboard service. You'll come up with something …

for next time

When you have time, prepare well in advance for anything that will help you make your decision more easily. For example:

- ▶ If you want the team to meet the candidates informally, organise this ahead so the team can make sure they're around for the interviews.
- ▶ If tests are going to help you, prepare for these in advance.
- ▶ If you're trying to fill a technical post and you're not a technical expert yourself, you could arrange for a more technically-minded colleague to spend a few minutes interviewing each candidate after you.

8 other types of interview

We've covered the standard selection interview, which is most likely what you're conducting at the moment. But it's possible that you may be running a slightly different type of interview – or you may need to in the future – so it's worth running through the guidelines for a few key interview types.

SECOND INTERVIEWS

When a job is a key one, you may occasionally find that you really cannot choose between two candidates after the initial round of interviews. I said earlier that you should aim to do the job properly first time, and so you should for a receptionist, a PR assistant or a sales executive. But more high-powered jobs are different. Often, two applicants will bring very different skills and it is hard to be sure which is the better choice.

But there's no point just repeating the interview you have already done. When you find yourself in this position, you need to call the candidates back in order to investigate their secondary skills in more depth and to identify their differing strengths. So you'll need to work hard to prepare a list of questions that will reveal more than the first interview's questions.

The other typical reason for holding second interviews is that you have produced a second shortlist of candidates who you consider are potential appointees, and someone else also needs to interview them with you. In this case, you will need to repeat many of the original questions for the benefit of your colleague.

PANEL INTERVIEWS

These are far more intimidating for the poor interviewee, so you need to work extra hard to make sure you put them at their ease. Don't make them sit alone on one side of a desk or table with all of you lot facing them across it. Sit in easy chairs if you can, or at least all sit round a table together. And make sure you tell the interviewee who you all are and your positions in the organisation.

You need to be well prepared (second nature to you, I'm sure); otherwise you can give a poor

PANEL SAFEGUARDS

Make notes individually at the end of each interview, and keep your own scoresheets, before you discuss the candidate with each other. Otherwise your views may be influenced by each other's, especially if someone has a particularly strong view about any of the candidates.

impression by being unsure who is asking what questions in what order. Divvy up the questions in advance, and follow a logical thread.

INTERVIEWING INTERNAL APPLICANTS

The way you handle internal applicants at interview is important. It is essential that they feel they are being treated fairly, and on an equal footing with other applicants. If they don't get the job, they will have to carry on working in the organisation, probably alongside the successful candidate (most internal applicants apply for jobs in their own department, or one they work with closely).

In order to treat internal applicants fairly:

▷ **Make their interview as formal as everyone else's, despite any temptation to be informal. If it doesn't feel like an interview to them, it won't feel right.**

- ▶ Give them as much time as everyone else, and don't answer their questions for them, or say, 'Of course, I know you can handle this, so we don't need to go into it.'

- ▶ Ask them exactly the same general questions as everyone else. These form your basis for assessing everyone against the same yardstick, so make sure your internal applicant has an equal opportunity to measure up to it.

- ▶ Don't assume they know more than they do about the job. It's safest to tell them exactly what you have told all the other candidates – they won't mind if some of it isn't news to them.

thinking smart

LETTING THEM DOWN GENTLY

Be especially considerate if you have to reject an internal applicant, and make sure you don't damage their confidence. Be as positive as you can and – above all – make sure they hear it from you first.

interview in
an evening

So the interviews are at nine o'clock tomorrow morning, and you haven't started on them yet? Whoops. Never mind: you can get yourself straight by morning, even if you have to spend most of this evening working. What you really need are a few tips for getting through this process as fast as possible.

- Before you leave the office, collect the following documents:

    - the application forms

    - the job description

    - the employee specification.

    Skim through the last two of these and check they still apply to the post (they may have been drawn up ages ago). If they don't, rework them so that they are accurate.

- If either the job description or the employee specification (or both) don't exist, you'll have to write one. This shouldn't take long; read Chapter 2.

- ▶ Also before you leave, make sure the receptionist and anyone else who needs to know is prepared for tomorrow's interviews. Promise them a list of candidates first thing in the morning, before the first one turns up (and make sure you remember to draw up the list). And check that your office, or whatever room you plan to use, will be available and set up for the morning.

- ▶ Write your list of general questions for all the applicants (see page 37) – you can do this before you go through the applications.

- ▶ Now go through the application forms, and make notes of the individual questions you want to ask each applicant (see page 38).

- ▶ Finally, read Chapter 6 on the interview itself before tomorrow morning.

- ▶ After the interviews are over, read Chapter 7 (on making the decision) before you finalise your choice.

What you really need are a few tips for getting through this process as fast as possible

interview in an hour

Uh-oh. An hour to go, and you've only just cleared the rest of the work out of the way. Now you have sixty minutes to turn the pile of application forms in front of you into a well prepared interview plan. You need Rumpelstiltskin. Failing that, you need to move fast. Very fast.

1 Read Chapter 1 so that you know what objective you're trying to achieve. When you're in a rush, you need a clear head more than ever.

2 To begin with, you need a job description and employee specification. If you don't have these on file – maybe this is a new post you're creating – you'll have to write them now (see Chapter 2). If someone is currently doing the job in question, and the job description and employee specification are out of date or non-existent, show them Chapter 2 of this book and ask them

to draft the documents for you in the next thirty minutes. Then you'll have to check them.

3 Now go through the applications. You shouldn't be doing this unless you already have the job description and employee specification in front of you, but this isn't the time to quibble. Use a highlighter pen to identify any specific areas that you want to question the candidate about – you don't have time to write out a list of questions.

4 Once you have a copy of the job description you can draw up a list of general questions to ask everyone (if you were lucky enough to have it from the start, it might be better to write these questions before you go through the applications). Take each of the key responsibilities on the job description and turn it into a question: 'One of the requirements of the job is [key responsibility]. What experience do you have in this area?'

5 Now do the same with the key attributes on the employee specification: 'This job calls for someone who can [key attribute]. Tell me what past experience you have of this.'

6 Finally, once you have your documents and your questions ready, arrange the room so that it is suitable for interviewing (see page 43).

You have sixty minutes to turn the pile of application forms in front of you into a well prepared interview plan

Now take a deep breath, relax, and get ready to smile and greet the first candidate warmly. They're on their way down the corridor now.

Take a deep breath, relax, and get ready to smile and greet the first candidate warmly